OCEAN OF LIFE

OCEAN OF LIFE

VISIONS OF INDIA AND THE

PHOTOGRAPHS BY MARILYN SILVERSTONE

PREFACE BY HAVEN O'MORE

AFTERWORD BY THE VEN. KHANPO THUPTEN

A
∀ SADEV
BOOK

APERTURE

HIMALAYAN KINGDOMS

STARS, A FAULT OF VISION, A LAMP, A PHANTOM, DEW, A BUBBLE.

A DREAM, A FLASH OF LIGHTNING, AND A CLOUD—

THUS WE SHOULD LOOK UPON THE WORLD.

DIAMOND-CUTTER SUTRA

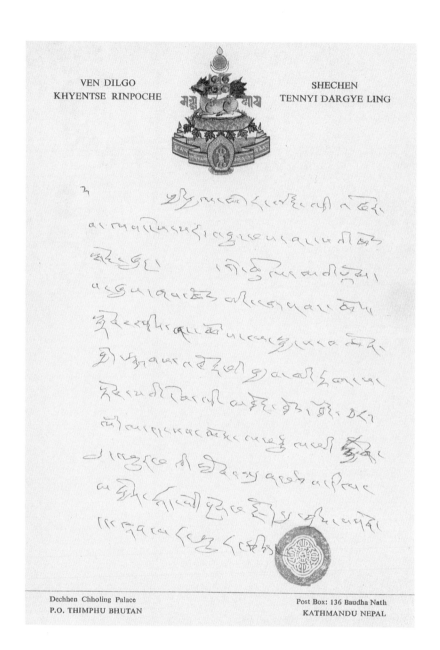

VEN DILGO
KHYENTSE RINPOCHE

SHECHEN
TENNYI DARGYE LING

Dechhen Chholing Palace
P.O. THIMPHU BHUTAN

Post Box: 136 Baudha Nath
KATHMANDU NEPAL

Marilyn, having become disenchanted with worldly life, entered the door of the Buddhadharma. She took the vows of a nun, receiving the ordination name Ngawang Chodron. While striving in the practice of Dharma she has made this book showing the impermanence of worldly affairs. For all who see or hear it, may this book become a cause of faith in the path of liberation and the means of turning them towards the supreme teaching. With this prayer the old man Dilgo Khyentse wrote this letter. May its purpose be accomplished.

INTRODUCTION

I went to India in 1959 for what was meant to be four months and stayed for fourteen years. I felt at home in India at once. Working as a photojournalist I thought it was important to record the history, the people, and all that I saw, and to preserve customs and ways of life that were disappearing. I was looking for something and I slowly discovered it through work and experiences. At the end of fourteen years it turned out to be Buddhism. I had always been attracted to Buddhism because of its all-embracing compassionate concern with all beings, from humans to the smallest gnat, its total non-exclusivity. I met Buddhism first in a prophetic way through an extraordinary Muslim woman who was a disciple of Mahatma Gandhi, Rehanaben Tyabji. I was drawn to it in the Himalayan kingdoms of Sikkim (which has since been absorbed into India), Nepal, and Bhutan. I formally became a Buddhist in 1973, just before leaving India.

These photographs are glimpses of the richness of life I found. Reflecting now on some of the photographs taken during those years, I see them colored with realizations I had before I knew them as the teachings of Buddhism, particularly impermanence.

In conceiving this book, I hoped to give people who had no contact with Buddhism a sense of it. Not everything in this book has turned out as I had originally envisioned. This in itself has been a good example of the teaching on impermanence and change. It is still my hope that perhaps those who see this book will pause, and begin to see things in a different way.

There are many people to thank: Chris and Constance Gianniotis of Shechen Tennyi Dargyeling in New York for unfailing support in all ways; Sonam Topgay Kazi for invaluable help interpreting the photographs of his native Sikkim; Sonam Paljor Denjongpa through whose interpreting in Sikkim in 1972 I first met and could speak to lamas, particularly the Venerable Khanpo Thupten who became and remains my first teacher and who has graciously written the afterword to this book; Buddhist friends who have pored over translations; and photographer friends who have generously lent encouragement. Looking back, there is no end to the chain of karmic connection leading to this moment.

At the head of all sentient beings who fill the vast realm of space, there are three people to whom I would like to offer whatever small merit there may be in composing this work. Like travelers met in a marketplace, they have departed to another life. Wherever they may be now in the vast ocean of life and death, I thank Elli Marcus, who taught me photography and started me on this path; Frank Moraes, without whom I could never have known India as I did; and the late Chogyal of Sikkim, Palden Thondup Namgyal, to whom I feel a karmic debt hard to repay.

Finally, this book is dedicated to His Holiness Dilgo Khyentse Rinpoche whose kindness is beyond words.

Marilyn Silverstone

PREFACE

We *forget* living in the Ocean of Life that we call this life. From the moment of birth, from the moment that we are born into this world we forget.

When we first open our eyes what do we see? We forget what we see. What is it that we first hear? We forget the first sounds that come to us. What do we first touch? Was it soft, our mother's flesh; was it hard, an instrument used during our birth; was it cold we felt, the air or water around us; was it hot, the sun's rays on us as our mother gave birth in the desert of life? Which was it for us of all these things, which appears to us?

We forget.

From this endless forgetting we construct our reality. Is it really *real?* Has it always been, has it been from the beginning, has it been from *before* the beginning? Has it always been and never been; has it always not never been and not not never been? Who can say this about "his" reality?

The Buddha, The One Awake can speak about *reality,* but not about "his" reality.

Suffering clings to the I, to the ego, to its or to his or to her this-ness or that-ness. To burn up the ego, the I, removes the pain of suffering. Then comes the *clearness;* then comes the *re-*membering; then comes the stopping of that wave upon wave of forgetting/suffering. The I attracts suffering more than a magnet attracts iron shavings.

The One Awake describes himself as unknowable: *here,* unassailable; *now,* unbecoming. "I wander the world a learned Nobody, uncontaminated by human-qualities; it is useless to ask my family name." Were this not the condition of all and available to all where would be its Truth? The signs of this world show its Truth: change and suffering and death as we move through the Ocean of Life and of Death.

These photographs before us lovingly taken over many years are a unique record, a *reminder* of this Truth. It is well that many will see these photographs; it is well that some may contemplate the texts placed throughout; it is well that Marilyn Silverstone searched for her duty, her *dharma,* and made the effort to bring its record to us.

"He who sees the Law (*dharma*) sees me," says The One Awake.

The One Awake taught the Law for the cessation of becoming, of change, of the *total* stopping of all suffering: here, this instant, forever, eternally and *beyond.*

Remember. Awake!

Haven O'More

Cambridge, Massachusetts. Written on the day the Buddha
awakened under the Bodhi tree, May 26, 528 B.C./1985 A.D.

Through ignorance, craving and becoming
Those born men, gods, and in the three inferior spheres,
Circle foolishly in the five realms of birth
Like the revolving of a potter's wheel.

Lalitavistara Sutra

Brother and sister grinding fodder. Mundia Khera village, Rajasthan, India, 1966.

Seeing the myriad forms of life there are,
acquiring human birth is as likely as becoming a universal king.
Among humans, to be of those who have faith in the teaching
is as rare as the coming of a Buddha.
Therefore always keep in mind this fortunate state.

Longchenpa

Village boys, Dewata village, Rajasthan, India, 1966.

Four farmers. Near Udaipur, Rajasthan, India, c. 1962.

The three worlds are impermanent as the clouds of autumn.
The births and deaths of beings are like watching a dance.
The speed of man's life is like lightning in the sky,
It passes swiftly as a stream down a steep mountain.

Karmaśataka Sutra

Schoolchildren waiting to hear newly-elected Indira Gandhi. Jaipur, Rajasthan, India, 1966.

Warli tribal girls looking over the boys at a temple fair. Mahalaxmi, Maharashtra, India, 1960.

Sweets seller at the annual Pushkar camel fair. Pushkar, Rajasthan, India, 1968.

By knowing that food is like medicine,
Rely on it without desire or aversion.
It is not for pride or self-aggrandizement,
It is not for increasing attractiveness,
But is only to support your body.

Suhrllekha

Prem Singh and his sons eating *makki-ki-roti* (cornmeal bread). Dewata Village, Rajasthan, India, 1966. Traditionally in India, women cook and serve the men, who eat alone.

The Ganga, especially, is the river of India, beloved of her people, round which are intertwined her racial memories, her hopes and fears, her songs of triumph, her victories and her defeats. She has been a symbol of India's age-long culture and civilization, ever-changing, ever-flowing, and yet ever the same Ganga. . . .

Smiling and dancing in the morning sunlight, and dark and gloomy and full of mystery as the evening shadows fall; a narrow, slow and graceful stream in winter, and a vast roaring thing during the monsoon, broad-bosomed almost as the sea, and with something of the sea's power to destroy, the Ganga has been to me a symbol and a memory of the past of India, running into the present, and flowing on to the great ocean of the future.

from the Will and Testament of Jawaharlal Nehru

Clad only in ashes and flowers, Hindu ascetics, or *Nagas,* lead two and a half million pilgrims to
the banks of the sacred Ganges, during the bathing festival of the Ardh Kumbh Mela. Allahabad, India, 1965.

Some are fettered by renouncing things;
Others by these same things gain unsurpassable enlightenment.
Saraha

Hindu ascetic, or *sadhu,* by the river Ganges. Allahabad, India, 1965.

Hindu holy men and their escort march to the Ganges during the festival of the Ardh Kumbh Mela.
Allahabad, India, 1965.

A veiled Muslim woman, wearing a *burqua,* in a crowd waiting to petition Mrs. Gandhi. New Delhi, India, 1966.

Sikh procession celebrating the 500th anniversary of Guru Nanak, founder of the Sikh Faith and first of its ten sainted Gurus. Old Delhi, India, 1969.

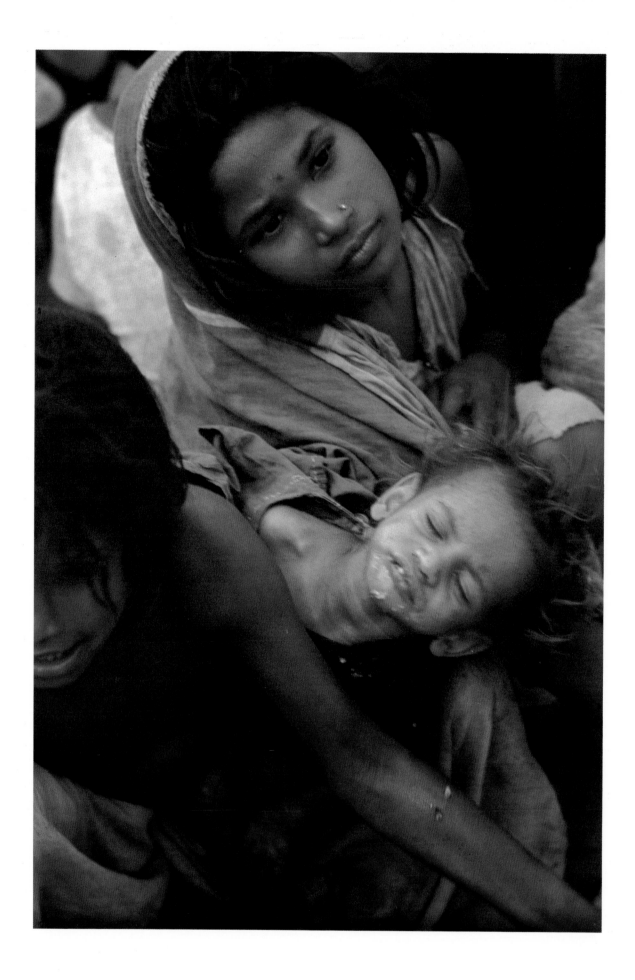

Girl and child at famine-relief food distribution. Bihar, India, 1967.

A *living being who in a previous life*
  has not been one's parent
Cannot be found, even by an omniscient mind.
All have cared for you, just as has
  your mother of this life.
Meditate on beings as having been your parents
  and remember their infinite kindness.

7th Dalai Lama

Mother and three children at government famine-relief works. Sadholi village, Raipur, Madhya Pradesh, India, 1966.

Harijan at a rally outside the Prime Minister's house, New Delhi, India, 1970. Mahatma Gandhi coined the name Harijan, meaning "People of God," for those previously called Untouchables.

The karma of beings
Is not exhausted even in a hundred kalpas.
Accumulating, when the time comes
The fruit of their good and bad actions ripens upon themselves.
Karmaśataka Sutra

The Ganges at Kalakankar. Uttar Pradesh, India, May, 1967. At dawn, before the sun rises to heat the air to 114°, villagers pray, bathe or relax on the high dunes of white sand.

Born on September 11, 1895, in Maharashtra, Acharya Vinoba Bhave was the spiritual heir of Mahatma Gandhi. Vinoba took a vow of celibacy at age ten and dedicated his life to the service of his country. He joined the Mahatma's ashram at Sabarmati, and at sixteen was made the head of a new ashram at Wardha. He went on to father India's Sarvodhaya (rural uplift) and Bhoodan (gift of land) movements. He walked more than 40,000 miles throughout his country, asking for gifts of land for the landless. In 1966, Vinoba was still walking, conducting the movement of Gramdan (gift of village). Gramdan represented a voluntary agreement by which villagers would deed ownership of their land to the community, retaining the right of cultivation. Five percent of each family's land would be donated to the landless. Thereafter, all village decisions would be made by consensus. Vinoba felt the urgency of awakening villagers to the concept of Gramdan self-help before they fell prey to other ideas. He died on November 15, 1982, at the age of eighty-eight.

He *who seriously wants to dispel*
all the misery of others
is an excellent man,
Because in the stream of his own being,
he has understood the nature of misery.
　　　　　　　　　　Jewel Ornament

Acharya Vinoba Bhave. Ranipatra Ashram, Bihar, India, 1966.

Villagers of Singhia Naya Tola, signing the deeds of Gramdan. Bihar, India, 1966.

Villagers heralding the arrival of workers of Vinoba's movement to their village which had joined Gramdan ten years earlier. Berain village, rural Bihar, India, 1966.

The palaces of impermanence
arise and disappear
together with the beings therein.
Jewel Ornament

Women in *purdah,* or seclusion, peer from windows in their quarter of the City Palace to see their prince during his marriage festivities. Jaipur, Rajasthan, India, 1966.

The Maharaja of Rajpipla is helped onto his horse as he prepares to enter the fort at Jaisalmer for his marriage to its princess. Rajasthan, India, 1964.

If when his time comes even a king should die
His wealth, friends and relatives cannot follow him.
Wherever men go, wherever they remain,
Karma, like a shadow, will follow them.

the Sutra called "Advice to a King"

Maharaja Sawai Man Singh of Jaipur and fellow maharajas lead the bridegroom's escort. Jaipur, Rajasthan, India, 1966.

The Maharaja of Rajpipla appears to the cloistered women of the palace the morning after his marriage to their princess. Jaisalmer, Rajasthan, India, 1964.

Even the glory and wealth of a universal monarch
Is like a festival enjoyed in a dream.
The activities of this life, though achieved by a hundred means
Must be abandoned, like a children's game.

                                        Tenpa'i Dron-mé

In the *zenana,* or women's quarters of the City Palace, the Maharani of Jaipur, in pink; the groom's sister, the Maharani of Baria; and other attendants, dressed in red, await the formal visit of the Prince before he leaves for his wedding. Jaipur, Rajasthan, India, 1966.

Rajput *thakurs,* or nobles, of Mewar at the annual feast during the celebration of Dussehra. Udaipur, Rajasthan, India, 1966. Mewar was the only state that never surrendered to the Moghul conquerors.

Bala's wedding. Chhawla village, Delhi, India, 1972. Shrouded in a white sheet and tied to her new husband, Bala waits to take the seven steps around the sacred fire which will make them man and wife.

Women calling guests to a wedding. Bundi, Rajasthan, India, 1964.

Hemantha's wedding. Bombay, India, c. 1961. Hemantha and Ashok Krishnadas feed each other after walking around the sacred fire.

Ever since the Moghul Emperor Akbar first entered the Valley four centuries ago, the Vale of Kashmir has been a summer resort for the rulers of India. In the 19th century the British followed the Moghuls' summer exodus to Kashmir and added houseboats, comfortable enlargements of the local living-barges and skiffs called shikaras, *which could be poled through the backwaters and anchored at will on a lakeside or on the embankment of the river Jhelum which winds through the city of Srinagar. Now, in Free India, tourists from home and abroad invade Kashmir in the summer months. In these few months the Kashmiris must do the business on which they live—ferrying tourists about in their* shikaras; *renting and servicing the houseboats; selling, with an ubiquitous urgency and persistence, Kashmir's abundance of flowers and fruits, painted papier mâché, intricately carved boxes and tables, and fabled finely-embroidered shawls that can be pulled through a ring.*

By November the chill settles in. Grey clouds roll in over the mountains and settle into the bowl of the valley. The tourists have gone—even the Kashmir government moves from Srinagar to Jammu, the winter capital in the plains, and the Kashmiris are left alone to see through the winter in their valley as best they can, sealed off sometimes for weeks from the outside world.

Few outsiders have ventured to Kashmir in winter, or recorded its life. For if in summer Kashmir belongs to others, in winter Kashmir belongs only to the Kashmiris and has its own true life, a cycle of somber beauty and poetry, of quiet endurance and icy, bone-penetrating cold.

At first samsara is a joyful experience.
Later its appearances are deceptive.
Finally, it is a prison without escape.
The Songs of Jetsun Milarepa

As snow starts to fall, two women and a child paddle their skiff towards shelter through the frozen backwaters of Dal Lake. Srinagar, Kashmir, 1968.

Barefoot, a young woman brushes the snow off her floating home, called a *doonga*, anchored in the frozen Jhelum river. Srinagar, Kashmir, 1968.

Tall brick and wooden houses loom in the bitter cold of a sunless winter afternoon. Srinagar, Kashmir, 1968.

Like cattle in the slaughterer's pen
Death is common to all
Yet even seeing the death of others
How is it you do not fear the Lord of Death?
                                        Aryadeva

Huddled against the snow and bitter cold, men gather in their skiffs for the weekly floating market. Srinagar, Kashmir, 1968.

Hungry dogs and crows attend the butchering of a sheep on the lake shore near the Hazratbal Mosque. Srinagar, Kashmir, 1968.

At the height of a blizzard, a youth breaks through the ice with his paddle. Srinagar, Kashmir, 1968.

All beings by nature are Buddha
as ice by nature is water.
Apart from water, no ice,
apart from beings, no Buddha.
                                    Hakuin

The head of a lotus, bent over by snow, lies imprisoned under water by a collar of ice. Dal Lake, Srinagar, Kashmir, 1968.

In Tibet we say that taming the mind is like "bridling a fine horse." A horse is a powerful animal, and if you do not have the means to control him properly he may gallop off wildly, possibly destroying himself and others as well. If you can harness that energy, however, the horse's great strength can be used for accomplishing many difficult tasks. The same applies to yourself. Looked at scientifically, your body, speech, and mind are nothing but varying forms of energy. Thus, if in the morning you direct this energy by strongly affirming your motivation, all the remaining energy of body, speech, and mind will follow in that same direction.

Internal feelings and sensations are aroused whenever we do any activity. When they come up, do not immediately think, "this is good" or "this is bad." Such automatic reactions only generate confusion, obscuring the reality of what is really happening. Instead, try to be mindful of all these feelings and sensations, and investigate them with introspective wisdom. This will develop in you the habit of alertness, making your mind clearer and less distracted.

Lama Yeshe

Horsemen gallop in a rough-and-ready polo game. Leh, Ladakh, 1969. The valley floor is 11,000 feet. The three white structures are *chotens,* Buddhist reliquaries whose shape symbolizes aspects of the enlightened mind.

*Look at the nature of the world
Impermanent, like a mirage or dream:
Even the mirage or dream does not exist.*
                              Tilopa

Fine summer rain falls on the apple trees and vegetable gardens of Lachen, as visitors climb to the monastery above. Lachen, North Sikkim, 1971.

Man holding blue *Meconopsis*. Near hot springs at Yumthang, North Sikkim, 1971.

*Even those who wish to find happiness and overcome misery
Will wander with no aim or meaning
If they do not comprehend the secret of the mind—
The paramount significance of the Dharma.*

Shantideva

Nomad carrying bags of salt across the high plateau of Ladakh behind the Himalayas. 1969.

Jeep decorated with the Nepalese flag, a portrait of King Mahendra, and poinsettias. Near Pokhara, Nepal, December, 1968. A long curtain of white cloud reveals a glimpse of Machha Puchhare, the Fishtail Mountain.

Graves marked with French, Chinese, and Indian names in a Roman Catholic cemetery. Mahe, Seychelles, 1967.

Indian army training at an altitude between 11,000 and 20,000 feet. Ladakh, 1969.

Doing no evil whatsoever
Practice virtue perfectly
Tame one's mind absolutely
This is the teaching of the Buddha.
                          Vinaya

Lama and acolytes surprised by visitors in the Lakhang Sarp (New Chapel) of the Tashichho Dzong. Thimphu, Bhutan, 1964. Tubular "Victory Banners" at left, called *gyaltsen,* symbolic of the Victory of Liberation won by the Buddha, hang in front of the altar. Founded in the 17th Century, the Dzongs are a series of great fortresses—part monastery, part administrative center. The Tashichho Dzong houses 1,000 state-supported monks in summer; in winter they move to the Dzong at the old capital of Punakha.

In the relative, things appear as in a dream
In the absolute, they have no solid existence,
Like an empty sky.

Kunkhyen Jigme Lingpa

Warrior dancers, attendants of the sacred Mt. Kangchenjunga and defenders of the Dharma, during the Sikkimese New Year Dances. Gangtok, Sikkim, 1968. The leader, right, wears on his shoulders the double dorje, symbol of invincibility. This is the only one of the Sacred Dances performed by laymen rather than monks. The performers must be in a pure state of mind before undertaking the dance. Its purpose is to raise the martial spirit needed to overcome evil.

Mask room of Pemayangtse Monastery. Western Sikkim, 1963. Each big monastery performs Sacred Dances once a year, presided over by the monastery's head lama, and attended by the public. The Dances are the means of "Liberation by Seeing," the personified psychodrama of dealing with ego. The ferocious masks are a preview of the visions of the after-death state, presented so that the viewer may recognize them in future as reflections of one's own mind and thus be liberated from fear.

Mind as such has no objectifiable reality, but for countless lifetimes we have not recognized this. As a result, we have given rise to the notion of a self, the notion "I." This notion "I" is the ego. It tends to create its own projections, to create a whole sphere of itself. This sphere is nothing other than the projection of ignorant ego, but we do not recognize this. Thinley Norbu Rinpoche

Pemayangtse Lama performing the Black Hat during Sikkimese New Year ceremonies. Gangtok, Sikkim, December 1963. Enacted at the end of the old year, this rite can only be performed by a spiritually attained Tantric lama, the "Vajra Master." Every detail of the costume has mystic power to resist the influence of evil spirits. The evil meant here is the demon of unmanageable ego. An effigy representing ego is enclosed in a straw "house" which is ignited after summoning the spirits. This is an example of *drak le*, compassionate action in the drastic form needed to handle a strong problem.

Carved and painted shrine at a wayside water source. Near Gangtok, Sikkim, February 1960. The letters spell the mantra of compassion, "Om Mani Padme Hung Hri"; the six colors represent the six regions of Samsara (worldly existence). Such shrines are meant to be a constant reminder of pure vision, speech, and mind, giving passersby a chance to earn good karma. The standing white figure is Chenrezig, the embodiment of the Buddha's compassion; the seated figure is of the Great Guru Padmasambhava, who visited Sikkim in the 8th Century and declared it one of the sacred "hidden lands"; the white *choten*, half visible at bottom left, represents the Enlightened Mind of the Buddha.

"By destroying evil, may all sentient beings attain enlightenment." The Pemayangtse lamas, who are also the royal priests, reciting prayers in conjunction with ceremonies performed by the Black Hat. Sikkimese-New Year, Gangtok, Sikkim, December 1963.

Doorway to the Lakhang Sarp, in the courtyard of the Tashichho Dzong. Thimphu, Bhutan, 1964. At the corners of the doorway, heroes on lotus pedestals support the beam and guard the entrance.

Try to understand how we perceive good and bad things in life according to our own delusions, our confused thoughts and conflicting emotions. We must try to understand that samsara is by nature impermanent, that things change constantly, that there are no solid entities to cling to. If we begin to look at the world in this way, then we can begin to generate inconceivable compassion toward all beings, with the thought of freeing them from suffering and confusion and fostering their happiness and peace of mind.

Dilgo Khyentse Rinpoche

Attended by the Abbot, the Venerable Trulshik Rinpoche, His Holiness Dilgo Khyentse Rinpoche blesses a nun of Thuptencholing Monastery. Thuptencholing, near Junbesi, Shar Khumbu, Nepal, December 25, 1976.

Long prayer banners, called *dar chok,* printed with mantras, flutter over cremation ground. Thimphu, Bhutan, 1964. Prayer flags fly wherever there are Buddhists in the Himalayas. When a person is cremated, up to 108 of these long banners are erected so that the air passing through them will spread their mantras throughout space for the benefit of the living and the dead. The finial represents the sword of wisdom, which cuts through ignorance to attain the Buddha Mind.

In general, whatever experiences you have,
   whether dreams or real,
If you cling to them as real, they will become
   an obstacle.
If you know them as illusion, they become the path.
                              The Songs of Lord Gampopa

The banner, called *Sridpa Ho,* is a diagram of the secret astrological mechanism that governs the physical world. Displayed at the start of any endeavor to avert adverse influences of worldly evil spirits, the banner will be carried at the head of the procession of lamas during Sikkimese New Year ceremonies. Gaṅgtok, Sikkim, 1963. Revealed on the belly of the Cosmic Tortoise, this astrological blueprint shows the structure of the physical forces of the universe according to Chinese astrology. The text exhorts: "Be transfixed by this: Do not be disturbed by what we do!"

Shrine containing a *Mani-chhukhor,* a wheel of prayers, turned by the stream running through it. Paro Kyerchu, Bhutan, 1964. A string of prayers printed on cloth has been hung on the shrine; the Bodhisattvas Manjushri, representing wisdom, and Chenrezig, representing compassion, flank the figure of Shabdrung Ngawang Namgyal, the 17th Century priest-statesman who unified Bhutan.

"Riding the horse of the wind, prayers multiply and spread through infinite space." Strings of small prayer flags, called *lung ta* (wind horses), sway and flutter in the mist. Near Enchay, Sikkim, 1971. Displaying the colors of the five elements, these flags are hung for happiness in the present and for the ultimate awakening into the Buddha nature.

AFTERWORD

This vessel for crossing Samsara's ocean of infinite suffering,
This hard to obtain ship of human birth, has been found
Through the Lama's kindness.
Remembering this kindness I pray again and again:
May all beings be blessed by seizing
The purpose of their existence in this lifetime.

To Tibet, the Land of Snows, many centuries ago, through their inconceivable kindness, Panditas and Masters brought the teachings of the Buddha, the "Six Ornaments and Two Superior Ones,"[1] and others, and translated them into Tibetan. Similarly, after that, Tibetan learned ones composed many commentaries on the Buddha's doctrine and teaching, which flourished to an extent the mind cannot encompass. This teaching, combining Sutra and Tantra, outlined a pure path, an unexcelled means to attaining liberation and the state of omniscience.

These days, many learned Tibetan lamas have been invited to many countries, East and West; and people of many kinds are studying Tibetan Dharma as well as medicine, psychology, art, and so forth.

Just as there are many kinds of medicine for a single kind of illness, for example, in this world there are many religions which preach how to achieve happiness for all beings. Though theories and ideas and ways of expressing them may differ, all seek to transform the "three doors" of body, speech, and mind of the practitioner, and teach the practice of kindness to others who just as ourselves do not wish suffering and desire happiness. Lying, slander, the work of the tongue, stealing, killing, and so forth—these sins of the body all agree must be abandoned. (Sadly, many people these days are fighting and raising weapons in the name of religion.)

In these times when there are the two sides—those who hold such belief and those who don't—it is most important that religious persons of different paths act in harmony with each other. By doing so, not only will the practitioners of these paths themselves flourish, but it will be of benefit—now and in the future—in achieving happiness for all beings.

It is most important from the beginning to understand the profound relationship of karmic cause and effect. If we do not know how the fruits of virtue and sin are the source of happiness and suffering, there is no way to develop the pure mind that wishes to attain the path of liberation.

All happiness and suffering—the source is one's own mind. Therefore, the Three Turnings of the Wheel of the Law, the doctrine spoken by the Buddha, all deal with the taming of the mind, the elimination of the "poisons" of anger, desire, and ignorance. In brief, as the Buddha taught:

Doing no evil whatsoever
Practice virtue perfectly
Tame one's mind absolutely
This is the teaching of the Buddha.

The Venerable Khanpo Thupten with his pupil, the Seventh Incarnation of the high lama Dzogchen Pema Rigdzin, Gantok, Sikkim, 1972.

What is the enlightened mind of caring for others? It is to have a kind mind towards all—high or low, good, bad, or indifferent—without thought of one's own benefit. It is not just to have a cherishing, loving mind towards one's own relatives, friends, wife or husband, children, dog, and so on.

Many of the people you see in the photographs in this book have gone on to their next life. Not one of us has any certainty that we may not suddenly die. At the time of death, even if a rich man has a treasury filled with gold, he is powerless to take as much as a grain of dust. This we all clearly understand. Therefore, at the time of having power over one's possessions, the best thing to do is to offer as much as one can to the preservation of the Dharma; the next best thing to do is help as much as one can those who are poor, suffering, and in need (these two acts will be useful for one's next life); and at the very least one should not hoard but use one's means for the needs of oneself and others. Without that, when the time comes that wealth and possessions have all been left behind, and naked and with empty hands folded across one's chest it is time to go on to the next life, it will be too late, even if one has regrets.

Thus, if one remembers impermanence, and takes refuge in the precious jewels of the Buddha's teaching, guarding in mind the inevitability of karmic cause and effect and developing a mind of helpfulness to others, all one's actions of body and speech become the means of following a Dharmic path.

The Venerable Khanpo Thupten

---

[1] Epithet for the eight great fathers of Mahayana Buddhist philosphical theory.

Ocean of Life is supported by a subvention from Institute of Traditional Science, Inc.

∀SADEV is a trade name owned by The Garden Ltd.

Aperture, a division of Silver Mountain Foundation, Inc., publishes a periodical, books, and portfolios of fine photography to communicate with serious photographers and creative people everywhere. A complete catalog is available upon request. Address: Aperture, 20 E. 23rd Street, New York City, New York 10010.

TEXT CREDITS Wherever possible we have traced the quotes and sutras that appear in this book to an original source. We reprint them through the kind permission of their publishers: p. 18 *The Life and Teaching of Naropa,* translated by Herbert Guenther (p. 206, paperback ed. 1971, Oxford University Press, Oxford, England); p. 23 *Songs of Spiritual Change* by Gyalwa Kalzang Gyats'o, the 7th Dalai Lama, translated by Glenn H. Mullin (p. 36, Snow Lion Publications, Inc., Ithaca, NY); p. 27 *The Jewel Ornament of Liberation* by Gampopa, trans. by Herbert Guenther (p. 97, 1970 ed., Rider and Company, London); p. 30 *The Jewel Ornament of Liberation* by Gampopa, trans. by Herbert Guenther (p. 43, 1970 ed., Rider and Company, London); p. 41 *The Rain of Wisdom* trans. by Nalanda Translation Committee under the direction of Chogyam Trungpa (p. 207, Shambhala Publications, Boulder, CO); p. 47 "Song of Zazen" by Hakuin Zenji quoted in *Taking the Path of Zen* by Robert Aitken (p. 112, North Point Press, San Francisco, 1982), all rights reserved; p. 48 *Wisdom Energy* from Lama Thubten Yeshe (pp. 126 and 138, Wisdom Publications, London); p. 52 *A Guide to Bodhisattva's Way of Life* by Shantideva trans. by Stephen Batchelor (p. 47, Library of Tibetan Works and Archives, Dharamsala); p. 60 *Echoes* by Ven. Thinley Norbu Rinpoche (p. 5); p. 67 "The Songs of Lord Gampopa" from *The Rain of Wisdom* (p. 233, Shambhala Publications, Boulder, CO).